AF592850

THE LONDON & BIRMINGHAM RAILWAY
150 Years on

THE LONDON & BIRMINGHAM RAILWAY 150 Years on

DAVID GOULD

David & Charles
Newton Abbot London North Pomfret (Vt)

British Library Cataloguing in Publication Data

Gould, David,
The London & Birmingham Railway 150
years on.
1. British Rail. *London Midland Region*
–History 2. Railways–England–
Midlands—History
I. Title
385'.09424 HE3020.L6

ISBN 0–7153–8968–8

Phototypeset in Linotron Futura
by Northern Phototypesetting Co, Bolton
and printed in Great Britain
by Redwood Burn Limited, Trowbridge
for David & Charles Publishers plc
Brunel House, Newton Abbot, Devon

Published in the United States of America
by David & Charles Inc
North Pomfret, Vermont 05053, USA

INTRODUCTION

Before the opening of the London & Birmingham Railway the fastest method of travel between the two cities was by mail coach at an average speed of almost 10 miles an hour. At the time this speed was considered to be very fast and was only achieved a few years before the railway opened.

The great impetus to increase the speed of road transport was the carriage of mail by stage coach introduced in 1784. By the turn of the century, the mail coaches which left London at 8 o'clock each evening were running at about 6 or 7 miles an hour. In an effort to speed up the mails, particularly to Ireland, Thomas Telford was commissioned to survey a road from London to Holyhead. His chosen Irish Mail route is followed by today's A5, Watling Street, as far as Weedon and then by the A45 to Birmingham.

In 1815 the Holyhead Road Act made provision for the appointment of commissioners and granted money to begin road improvements. By 1837, when the first section of the railway opened, over two hours had been cut off the road journey from London to Stony Stratford.

In the early nineteenth century most of the capital's coal was still carried by sea, but an increasing amount of cargo was being transported from London to Birmingham by canal. The first waterway link between the two cities had been opened in July 1790 and consisted of a circuitous route via the Thames navigation, the Oxford, Coventry, and Birmingham & Fazeley canals. This route quickly proved to be unsatisfactory and the construction of the Grand Junction Canal was proposed. In 1793 work began on the new waterway to link the Thames at Brentford with the Oxford canal at Braunston. Most of the canal had been completed in 1800 when the Warwick & Birmingham and Warwick & Napton canals opened, further shortening the route into Birmingham. The completed canal route was opened officially with all due ceremony on 25 March 1805.

With such a large investment in new roads and canals between London and Birmingham, it is not surprising that the road coach and canal proprietors viewed the prospect of a competing railway link with great hostility. Some preparatory work in arranging finance for a railway was carried out in 1823. But the first positive steps were taken in January 1824 when Sir John Rennie began to survey a proposed railway route. The canal companies were thrown into disarray and their share values plummeted. Financial problems also struck the railway project and, although another survey was carried out, this time by Francis Giles, the plans were put into abeyance. It was not until 1829 that proposals for two competing lines by rival companies were published. One was along the route recommended by Rennie through Oxford and Banbury, the other on the line advocated by Giles through Rugby and Coventry.

In the summer of 1830 the two companies decided to join forces and employ George and Robert Stephenson to report on both surveys. A decision was quickly made in favour of the eastern route and on 18 September 1830 George Stephenson & Son were retained to carry out a detailed survey. Both Rennie and Giles, having carried out the initial surveys, mounted a campaign against the employment of the Stephensons.

Despite fierce opposition from supporters of Rennie and Giles, Robert Stephenson and his assistant Tom Gooch undertook the first surveys in the autumn of 1830 and completed them during the following year. The London & Birmingham Railway Bill with plans of the proposed line were presented to Parliament in 1832 and were accepted by the Commons. However, the proposals were rejected by the House of Lords on 19 June in the same year.

There had been considerable opposition to the railway particularly from landowners along the proposed route and those involved in road and canal transport. But the opposition from the landowners quickly disappeared when Stephenson carried out a further survey and offered up to three times the original value for the purchase of land. After buying off the landowning opposition, the second bill, which detailed a terminus at Chalk Farm and not Euston, was quickly accepted by Parliament and received the Royal Assent on 6 May 1833.

The Act and plans describe the route of the proposed railway and lists the owners and occupiers of land and property through which the line was to pass.

Among the many provisions of the Act, there are the requirements that the track gauge should not be less than 4ft 8in and the outside edges of the rails were not to be more than 5ft 1in apart. The carriages were to be constructed as directed by the company and only engines approved by the company were to be used on the railway. There was also the provision that all locomotives and stationary steam engines should consume their own smoke and there was a penalty of £5 to be paid by any offender. The railway was not permitted to cross any turnpike roads on the level and the company was required to erect crossing gates where the line crossed ordinary highways.

Although the London & Birmingham Act was passed in May 1833 it was not until 20 September that Robert Stephenson was appointed engineer for the construction of the railway. He quickly assembled his staff and they began staking out the course of the line in November 1833.

The construction of the railway, just over 112 miles long, involved civil engineering works on a scale never before seen in this country. For administrative purposes the line was divided into London and Birmingham divisions. These divisions were each divided into two engineering districts each in the charge of an assistant engineer and sub assistants. Each district was further divided into a number of sections. Contracts were let for the construction of each section and, in addition, there were separate contracts for particularly difficult cuttings, tunnels and viaducts.

The first contract to be started, in June 1834, was for the 5¾ mile Primrose Hill section including the 3,492ft tunnel. Within five months the contractor had been defeated by the difficult excavation conditions and Stephenson took control of the work. He improved and strengthened the stability of the tunnel by including an inverted arch below track level. Eventually the Primrose Hill contract was completed at a total cost of over £280,000, more than double the original contract price. It was a sorry story which was repeated at almost all other major construction projects on the line.

In July 1835 a further Act authorised the extension of the line from Chalk Farm to a terminus at Euston. By the autumn of 1835, despite the excavation difficulties already experienced, all of the construction contracts had been let.

Euston station was opened on 20 July 1837 and a service to Boxmoor (Hemel Hempstead) introduced. Difficulties in the completion of the major engineering works at Tring, Blisworth and Kilsby delayed the official opening of the line throughout until 17 September 1838.

Having completed the construction work, Stephenson was retained by the company as a consultant. One problem which continued to concern him for several years was the settlement of soil in the embankments and cuttings. Another source of trouble was the design of the railway track.

Individual stone blocks 2ft square were used to support the iron rails on most of the line. The rails were kept in gauge by iron tie rods. Wooden cross sleepers were used, but only over ground subject to settlement. Several experiments were carried out to find the safest and most economical spacing for the expensive stone blocks but there were still many occasions when the rails spread apart.

At Birmingham the Curzon Street terminus was shared with the Grand Junction Railway which provided an onward link to Liverpool and Manchester. But the London & Birmingham Railway remained as an independent company until 1846 when it was joined by the Manchester & Birmingham and the Grand Junction to form the London and North Western Railway.

The facilities at Euston quickly became overwhelmed by rapidly increasing passenger traffic. New lines were being opened, and the connection from Hampton-in-Arden to Derby provided, expanding links to the North East. To increase passenger capacity, the first alterations and additions were soon made to the original buildings, a process of piecemeal reconstruction which was to continue for over a hundred years.

The same overcrowding was soon experienced at Curzon Street, Birmingham. However, the confined station site and inadequate position made finding a solution here more difficult. Eventually, a new through station, largely designed by Robert Stephenson, was built on a new site adjacent to the city centre and opened in 1854. Named New Street, the station was later extended considerably but never became a confused jumble like Euston.

The heavy increase in traffic was also causing congestion on the railway and an additional up track was completed between Bletchley and Primrose Hill in 1859. A second down track to Bletchley was added in 1876. Permission was later granted to extend the two additional tracks northwards to Roade and from there to Northampton, rejoining the original route at Rugby.

Around the turn of the century, the LNWR provided some inner suburban London services. However, limited track capacity and old signalling methods restricted their provision on the main line route until the construction of what were known as the New Lines to Watford. Two additional tracks and new small stations were provided for suburban services first opened between Kensal Green tunnel and Harrow on 15 June 1912, extending to Watford on 10 February 1913. Development of the lines towards Euston involved the construction of a new tunnel at Primrose Hill and burrowing non-conflicting junctions at Chalk Farm to segregate Broad Street and Euston traffic. At first services on the New Line were steam, but electric trains began running to Broad Street via the spur at Willesden and the North London line, and to and from the Bakerloo Line during the first World War. The complete electric service to Broad Street (via Chalk Farm) and Euston did not start until 1922.

From then on the line continued largely unchanged other than in motive power until the massive main line electrification scheme of the 1960s. Old Euston, including its massive entrance archway, was demolished to make way for the modern concrete and glass structure in use today. Bridges and other structures throughout the route were altered to clear the way for overhead electric wires. Individual small signalboxes were removed and replaced by large power-operated boxes sited at strategic points along the line to control the new colour-light signalling system over long distances.

However, after all the changes, the route of the London & Birmingham Railway, with its massive earthworks, still remains as a reminder of Stephenson and the men who built it. The modern photographs in this book were all taken after June 1984, exactly 150 years after work started on the first contract to construct the first main line railway into London, the London & Birmingham Railway.

London–Birmingham Expresses

From the opening of its railway, the L&B and later the LNWR fiercely defended its monopoly of London–Birmingham traffic. But, after several years of opposition, the Birmingham & Oxford Railway opened in 1852 giving the Great Western a through route from London to Birmingham.

Almost immediately the Great Western began its battle for traffic by introducing a 2hr 45min service between Paddington and Snow Hill. At the time the fastest LNWR services were taking three hours. However the GWR soon revised its schedules in line with the LNWR timings. Then in 1859 two expresses were introduced by Paddington which cut 10 min off the Euston timings. But again these services lasted only a short time.

Further attempts were made to speed up the services in subsequent years, but Paddington could not compete when the LNWR introduced a non-stop 2hr 5min service on 2 June 1902. This was further improved to two hours from 1 March 1905. For five years the LNWR two hour service reigned supreme in an unassailable position. Then the GWR struck back.

On 1 July 1910 the journey from Paddington to Snow Hill was reduced from 129.3 miles to 110.6 miles by the opening of the Bicester cut-off. From then on, Paddington and Euston could compete on almost similar terms.

Between the wars, the two hour express was the general order of the day for both lines, but in 1935, there was another small skirmish. On 30 September the LMS began a 1hr 55min service from Euston when it introduced the new Jubilee class locomotives to the Birmingham services. In retaliation, the GWR prepared plans to introduce a 1hr 45min service. The threatened battle however, did not materialise and express timings remained at around two hours until 1939.

From the outbreak of war, train timings increased considerably and as early as October 1939 the fastest scheduled Euston–Birmingham time was 2hr 41 min. War damage and lack of maintenance took their toll on fast running and it was not until 1957 that the pre-war timings were reintroduced.

As soon as the decision had been made to electrify the Euston services it was obvious that the Paddington route would be at a serious disadvantage. Eventually the Paddington trains were diverted back to the original route via Oxford and with additional calls timings increased to 2hr 40min. Electrification of the Euston–Birmingham route brought express services every half an hour with minimum timings of just over 1½ hours.

Signalling

The demonstration of an electric telegraph system between Euston and Camden in 1838 could have heralded the first application of electrical science for controlling the movement of trains. That honour, however, fell to the Great Western in the following year when the equipment, devised by Wheatstone and Cooke, was installed between Paddington and West Drayton.

Throughout its line, the London & Birmingham used flag and board signals by day and coloured lights at night. But a pneumatic tube with trumpets was used to control the operation of the cable haulage system which was used to pull trains up the incline and lower them down between Euston and Camden. On the rest of the route there was no communication between individual signalmen, or, as they were known at first, policemen, and the time interval system was used in the hope of keeping trains a safe distance apart.

The policeman was required to stand erect and give no flag signal if the line ahead was clear. Caution was required if a train had passed on the same line within five minutes and was indicated by a green flag held up at 45 degrees. Caution due to defective rails was indicated by the green flag being held down at 45 degrees. To stop a train the policeman would show a red flag. At night a white lamp indicated a clear line, a green lamp caution and a waving red lamp was used to stop a train.

Signalling posts with red and green boards were provided at each station and at each end of Primrose Hill, Watford and Kilsby tunnels. After a train passed through a station without stopping, the green board was displayed for ten minutes. If the train stopped, a red board was displayed for five minutes after the train's departure and then a green board was shown for a further five minutes. A red signal was shown for ten minutes after a train had entered a tunnel. If the policeman could see that the train had cleared the tunnel, a green board would be displayed for the remainder of the ten minutes. At night, red and green lamps replaced the coloured boards.

Engine drivers were required to keep a good look-out and not exceed their normal speed or run before their proper time. They were also ordered to stop at a red board or light and proceed with caution after passing a green signal. Engines were also required to carry white or coloured boards or lights to indicate their specific duty.

Originally the policeman walked round and operated his various boards or lights individually. The first attempt to operate several signals from one operating position remotely from a signalling shelter is said to have been accomplished unofficially by a policeman at Watford in 1846.

The introduction of the electric telegraph on the main lines during the late 1850s enabled policemen to communicate with each other and the time interval system of operation became less liable to dangerous situations. The system was known as the two-mile telegraph since the telegraph stations were roughly two miles apart. For another 25 years trains were still allowed to proceed into an occupied section under what was called permissive block. Not until the early 1880s did the LNWR adopt the absolute block system which permitted only one train in a block section at one time, for passenger trains, which became a legal requirement in 1889.

By then, the signal and point levers together with the telegraph controls and interlocking systems had been gathered together at intervals along the route and enclosed in signalboxes. The line was therefore split into signalling sections each under the control of a signalbox, providing the basic system of train regulation which operated on the line for over one hundred years.

Some modification was carried out after the turn of the century when an electrically operated system developed by LNWR engineers Webb and Thompson was installed at Crewe and one or two other areas, including Camden just outside Euston. Semaphore signals and discs were operated by solenoids and points moved by electric motor. At Euston there were few improvements to the signalling until 1952 when a new power signalbox opened with electric lever operation, track circuits, colour-light signals and electro-pneumatic points. However, the new signalling system and signalbox had only a short life for they were completely superseded by a new centralised signalbox installed as part of electrification in the early 1960s. At the same time colour-light signals were installed in stages throughout the Euston–Birmingham route together with continuous track circuiting. Individual small signalboxes were replaced by seven power operated signalling centres at Euston, Willesden Junction, Watford Junction, Bletchley, Rugby, Coventry and Birmingham. The Rugby signal-box alone with all its main line connections controls a total of 59 route miles, and replaced 22 old signal-boxes. Development of remote control systems of communication has continued and an optical fibre high capacity control link was installed experimentally between Coventry and Birmingham in the early 1980s.

Despite all the advances in modern signalling methods, one small signal cabin still exists on the main route into London. Tucked away in the lonely Northamptonshire countryside at Banbury Lane, the crossing barriers and associated signals are still operated from the small brick and timber signal box beside the line.

Along the route

From the platform end at Euston, the start of the steep incline up to Camden can be seen as the track rises up beyond Hampstead Road bridge. The electric locomotives of today seem to glide almost effortlessly up the climb which in the past has sorely tested many steam engines. The ear splitting eruption of smoke and steam, the furious roar of wheel slip and the struggling rear bank engine have now been replaced by quiet, apparently undemanding, acceleration.

Just beyond the top of Camden bank on the right, can be seen the original roundhouse engine shed of the London & Birmingham Railway (today a theatre) and Primrose Hill station with the connection of the North London Railway. A small yard on the left for stabling parcels vans now marks the site of Camden locomotive shed. Primrose Hill tunnel is soon passed and on the right South Hampstead station, the first station to be reached on the New Line. On the up side, after Kensal Green tunnel, is Willesden traction depot, followed almost immediately by the site of Willesden Junction station. On the down side is the Freightliner depot built on the site of the original Willesden sheds. Beyond, on the right, several locomotives can usually be seen in sidings before the marshalling yard and carriage servicing depot are reached.

With smooth acceleration from Willesden, the trains pass through Wembley Central at full speed, below the High Road shopping centre. Small suburban stations on the New Line are passed on the left before the decorative brickwork of the LNWR Harrow & Wealdstone station comes into view.

The dc conductor rail lines turn to the west as the main line reaches Bushey, and rejoin the main route just south of Watford Junction. Almost hidden behind a retaining wall on the up side, just north of Watford station, is the London & Birmingham original station building. The fast and slow lines divide to pass through the two bores of Watford tunnel, joining again to run beside the Grand Union Canal on the climb of over 16 miles through the Chilterns to Tring. A short level run precedes the steady down gradient through the deep, grass covered chalk of Tring cutting. The chimneys of a large cement works indicate the end of the cutting and within a short distance the woodland hills of Ivinghoe Beacon rise up on the eastern skyline.

Through Cheddington the falling gradient continues but rises shortly to fall again through Leighton Buzzard and the three bores of Linslade tunnel. Brickworks to the east and a concrete flyover mark the approach to Bletchley. The branch to Bedford curves to the east away from the main line just north of the station and the glass, metal and concrete multi-coloured buildings of Milton Keynes soon come into view. The dual carriageway of the A5 road accompanies the line through the new city with its Central station building high above the tracks.

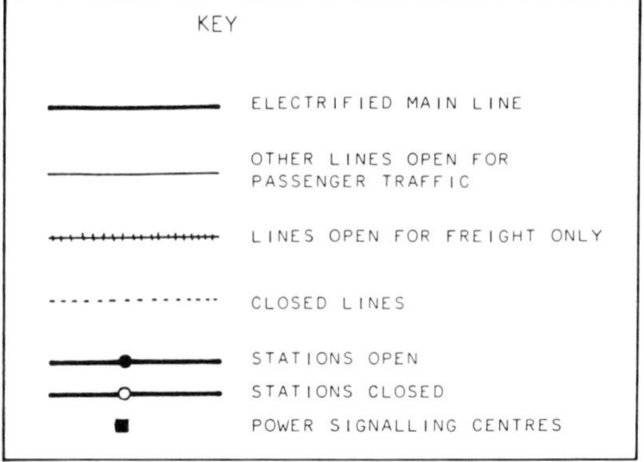

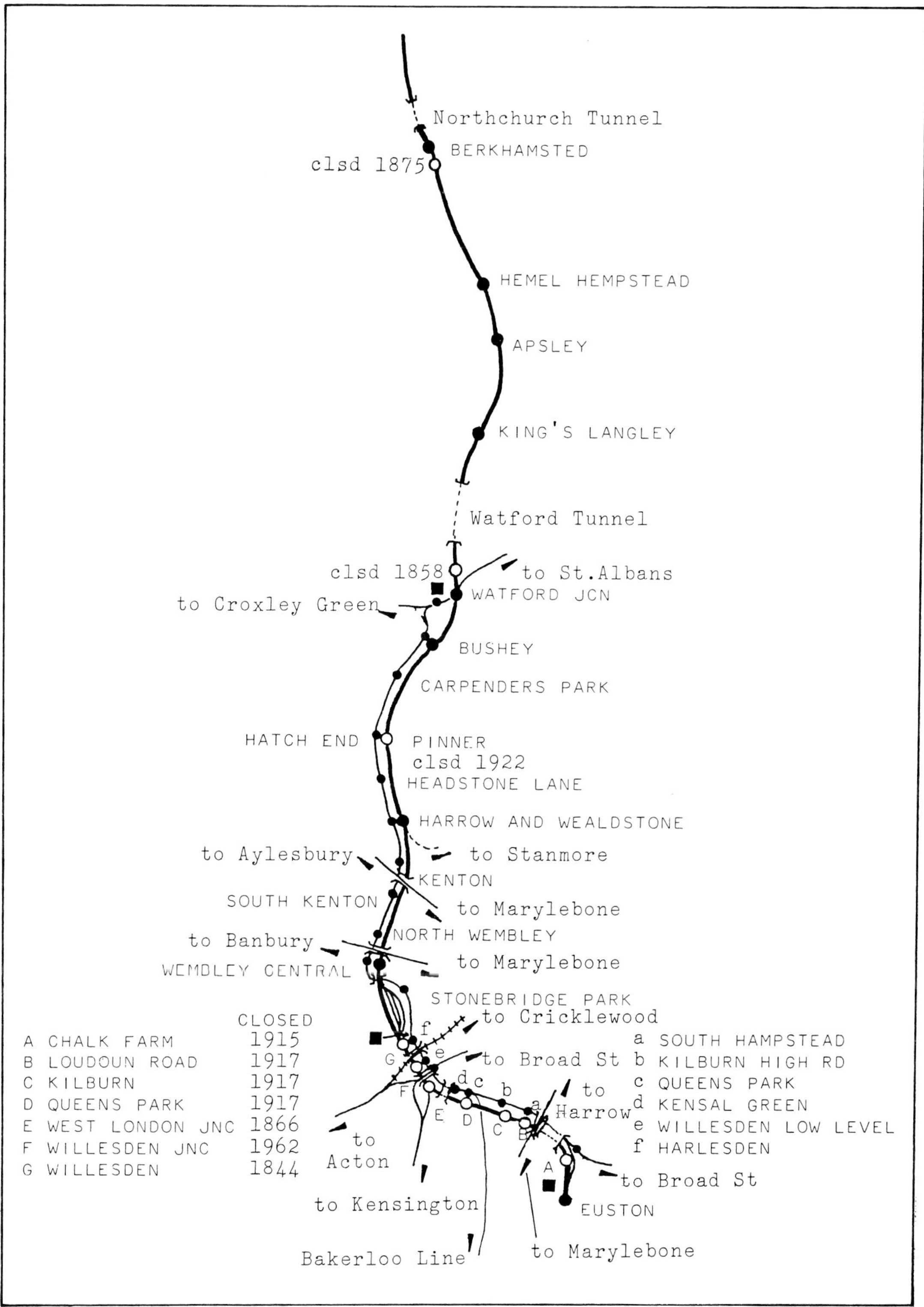
Northchurch Tunnel
BERKHAMSTED
clsd 1875
HEMEL HEMPSTEAD
APSLEY
KING'S LANGLEY
Watford Tunnel
clsd 1858
to St.Albans
WATFORD JCN
to Croxley Green
BUSHEY
CARPENDERS PARK
HATCH END
PINNER
clsd 1922
HEADSTONE LANE
HARROW AND WEALDSTONE
to Aylesbury
to Stanmore
KENTON
SOUTH KENTON
to Marylebone
NORTH WEMBLEY
to Banbury
WEMBLEY CENTRAL
to Marylebone
STONEBRIDGE PARK
to Cricklewood
CLOSED
A CHALK FARM 1915
B LOUDOUN ROAD 1917
C KILBURN 1917
D QUEENS PARK 1917
E WEST LONDON JNC 1866
F WILLESDEN JNC 1962
G WILLESDEN 1844
a SOUTH HAMPSTEAD
b KILBURN HIGH RD
c QUEENS PARK
d KENSAL GREEN
e WILLESDEN LOW LEVEL
f HARLESDEN
to Broad St
to Harrow
to Acton
to Broad St
EUSTON
to Kensington
Bakerloo Line
to Marylebone

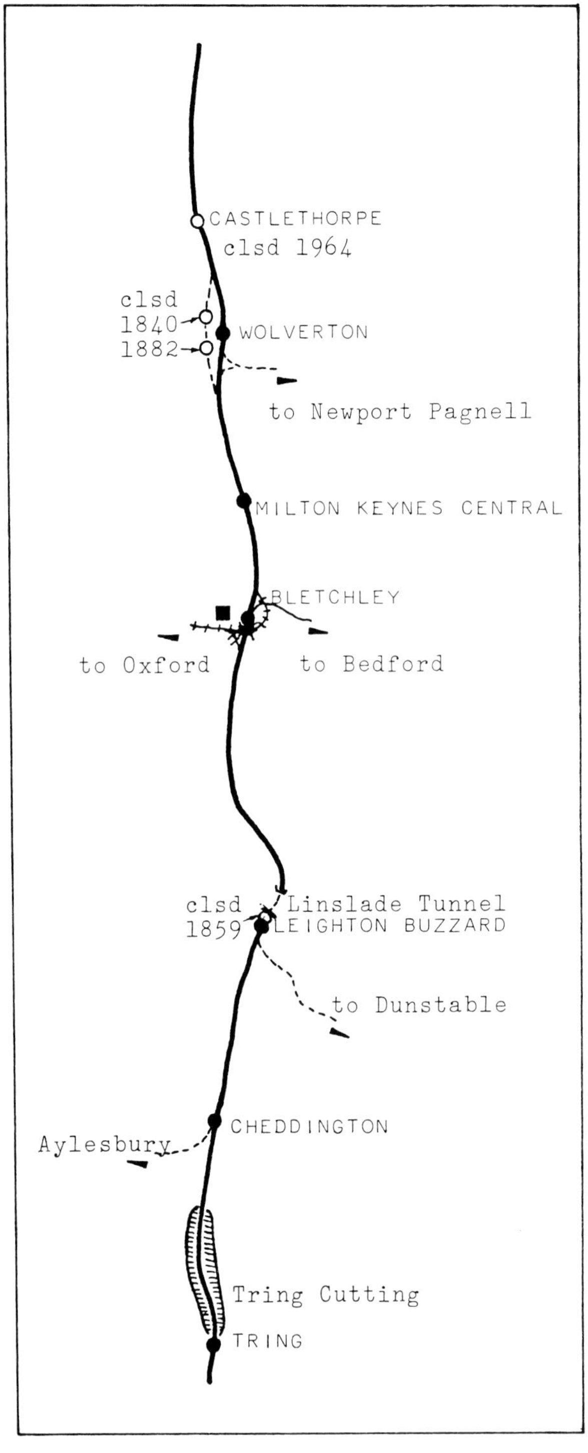

The line curves to the east away from its original line on the approach to Wolverton to pass round the carriage works buildings. North of the station, the line curves back to the west on to its original course to pass over the impressive Ouse viaduct. Climbing out of the Ouse valley the line soon reaches Castlethorpe and then on to Roade and the deep cutting through the Northamptonshire Upland. Huge blue brick retaining walls line the sides of the cutting at its deepest section. The slow lines drop down below reinforcing steel work to turn sharply off at the north end of the cutting towards Northampton.

At the site of Blisworth station, the line is again joined by the Grand Union Canal for an almost level run of over three miles. Stowe Hill tunnel, scene of two serious accidents, marks the approach to Weedon with its now empty military establishment. Within a couple of miles the railway and canal are joined on their northward path by the roaring traffic on the M1 motorway. The canal soon meanders off to the left but the railway and road run closely parallel on towards Watford Gap. Turning back under the railway, the canal snakes northwards towards Leicester as the motorway and railway diverge at the site of Welton station.

A short level stretch precedes the plunge through the long Kilsby tunnel. Light from the two large, 60ft diameter, ventilation shafts, dimly illuminate the darkness of the tunnel, a reminder of the fears experienced by some when such a long tunnel was first proposed.

A fly-over junction with the slow lines and the steel girders of the old Great Central bridge herald the entrance to Rugby with its one large island platform. The lines then turn to the west, past sidings and junctions, the down line taking its original alignment but the up line climbing up over the Trent Valley line on a concrete fly-over. Joined again after the complications of Rugby, the two tracks run down through the site of Brandon & Wolston to climb again towards Coventry. The line from Leamington and the Western Region swings in tightly from the

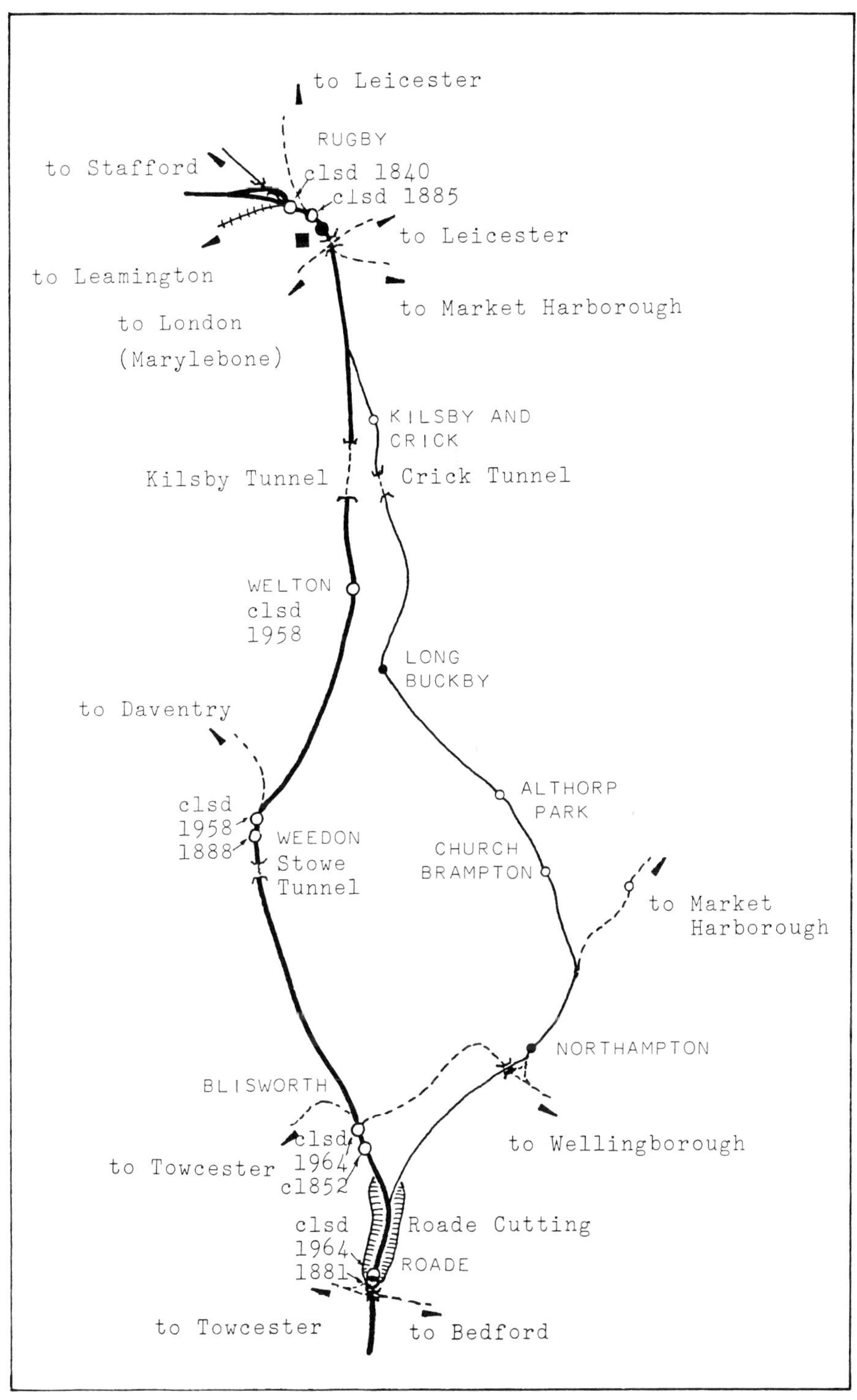
to Leicester
RUGBY
to Stafford
clsd 1840
clsd 1885
to Leicester
to Leamington
to Market Harborough
to London
(Marylebone)
KILSBY AND
CRICK
Kilsby Tunnel
Crick Tunnel
WELTON
clsd
1958
LONG
BUCKBY
to Daventry
ALTHORP
PARK
clsd
1958
1888
WEEDON
Stowe
Tunnel
CHURCH
BRAMPTON
to Market
Harborough
NORTHAMPTON
BLISWORTH
clsd
1964
c1852
to Towcester
to Wellingborough
Roade Cutting
clsd
1964
1881
ROADE
to Towcester
to Bedford

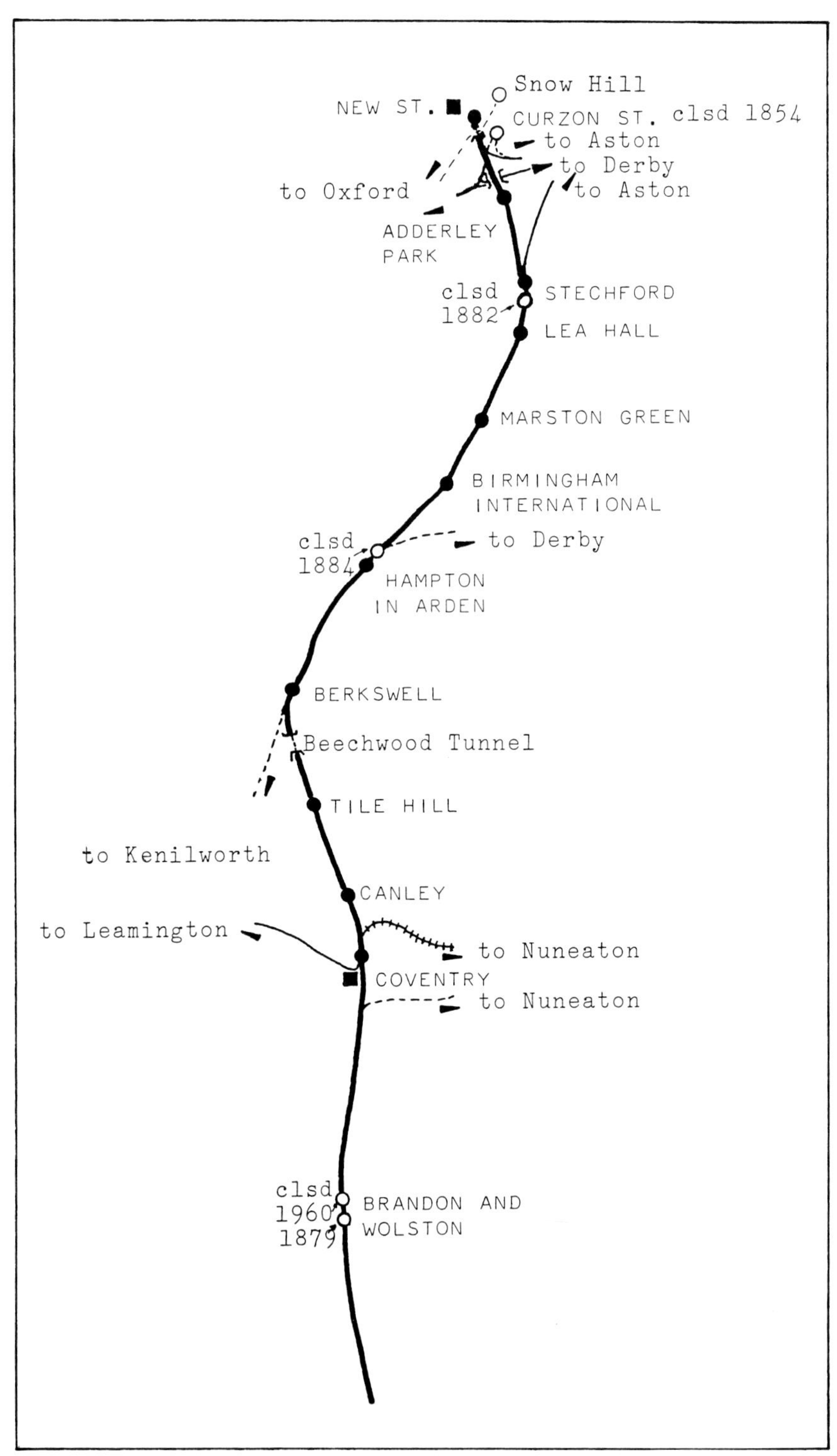
Snow Hill
NEW ST.
CURZON ST. clsd 1854
to Aston
to Derby
to Aston
to Oxford
ADDERLEY
PARK
clsd
1882
STECHFORD
LEA HALL
MARSTON GREEN
BIRMINGHAM
INTERNATIONAL
clsd
1884
to Derby
HAMPTON
IN ARDEN
BERKSWELL
Beechwood Tunnel
TILE HILL
to Kenilworth
CANLEY
to Leamington
to Nuneaton
COVENTRY
to Nuneaton
clsd
1960
1879
BRANDON AND
WOLSTON

south on the approach to Coventry station. A large car park marks the site of the once busy goods sheds as the line climbs away from Coventry to reach the summit at Beechwood tunnel.

Several small suburban stations are passed in quick succession until the large rectangular blocks of the National Exhibition Centre come into view to indicate arrival at Birmingham International. An overhead MAGLEV transportation system links the railway station with the adjacent international airport.

The line to Aston, Walsall and the north avoiding Birmingham runs off to the north west as the main line turns to the west at Stechford. Through cuttings of over a mile in length and through Adderley Park station, the line is joined by tracks from the north, east, south and west at Grand Junction. On the up side can be seen the extensive Lawley Street Freightliner yard and within a short distance, beyond the distinctively marked Post Office Parcels Depot, is the original L&B terminus at Curzon Street. Climbing steeply, the line rises up through South tunnel to arrive at New Street station below the massive deck construction of the Birmingham Shopping Centre.

Chronology

6 May 1833	London & Birmingham Railway Act passed, for a railway from Chalk Farm London to Curzon Street Birmingham.
3 July 1835	London & Birmingham Railway Act authorised the extension of the line to Euston.
20 Jul 1837	Railway opened from Euston to Boxmoor.
9 April 1938	Line extended from Boxmoor to Denbigh Hall (between Bletchley and Wolverton) and the Rugby to Birmingham section opened. Passengers conveyed by road coach between Denbigh Hall and Rugby.
24 June 1838	Some limited through working from London to Birmingham began.
17 Sept 1938	Official opening of the London & Birmingham Railway.
10 June 1839	Aylesbury Railway, Cheddington to Aylesbury opened. Closed 2 Feb 1953 passengers, 2 Dec 1963 goods.
12 Aug 1839	Stonebridge Railway, Hampton in Arden to Whiteacre opened. Original route towards Derby and North East. Closed 1 Jan 1917 passengers, 24 Apr 1930 goods.
1 Jul 1840	Midland Counties Railway, Rugby to Leicester opened. Provided links to Derby, York, Newcastle. Closed 1 Jan 1962.
27 May 1844	West London Railway. Willesden to Kensington opened.
9 Dec 1844	Warwick & Leamington Union Railway, Coventry to Warwick (Milverton) opened. Closed 18 Jan 1965 passengers, reopened 2 May 1977.
2 Jun 1845	London & Birmingham Railway, Blisworth to Peterborough opened throughout. Closed 4 Jan 1960, Blisworth to Northampton passengers, 6 Jul 1964 goods.
18 Jul 1846	London & Birmingham Railway with the Grand Junction and the Manchester & Birmingham railways became the London & North Western Railway.
17 Nov 1846	Bedford Railway, Bletchley to Bedford opened.
30 Nov 1847	Trent Valley Railway, Rugby to Stafford opened.
29 May 1848	Dunstable Railway, Leighton Buzzard to Dunstable opened for goods, 1 Jun 1848 passengers. Closed 2 Jul 1962.
29 Apr 1850	LNWR, Rugby to Market Harborough opened. Closed 6 Jul 1964 goods, 6 Jun 1966 passengers.
1 May 1850	Buckinghamshire Railway, Bletchley to Banbury opened. Closed Bletchley to Buckingham 7 Sept 1964 passengers, 5 Dec 1966 goods.
12 Sept 1850	LNWR, Coventry to Nuneaton opened. Closed 18 Jan 1965 passengers.
15 Feb 1851	East & West India Docks and Birmingham Junction Railway (North London Railway), junction made with LNWR at Hampstead Road.

1 Mar 1851	LNWR, Rugby to Leamington opened. Closed 15 Jun 1959 passengers.
20 May 1851	Buckinghamshire Railway, Bletchley to Oxford opened. Closed 1 Jan 1968 passengers.
15 Feb 1853	North & South Western Junction Railway, Willesden to Kew opened for goods, 1 Aug 1853 passengers.
1 Jun 1854	Birmingham New Street opened.
1 Jul 1854	Birmingham Curzon Street closed for normal traffic.
5 May 1858	LNWR, Watford to St Albans opened.
1 Jul 1858	Main line tracks widened. Third line (up goods) completed between Watford and Primrose Hill.
1859	Third line extended to Bletchley.
2 Jan 1860	Hampstead Junction Railway, Willesden to Camden opened.
1 Oct 1862	Watford & Rickmansworth Railway, Watford to Rickmansworth opened.
1 May 1866	Northampton & Banbury Junction Railway, Blisworth to Towcester opened. Closed 7 Apr 1952 passengers, 3 Feb 1964 goods.
2 Sept 1867	LNWR, Wolverton to Newport Pagnell opened. Closed 7 Sept 1964.
1876	Main line tracks widened. Fourth line (down goods) completed between Bletchley and Primrose Hill.
1879	Second bore of Primrose Hill tunnel completed and the two additional lines extended to Euston.
7 Sept 1880	LNWR, Stechford to Aston opened goods, 1 Mar 1882 passengers.
1 Aug 1881	LNWR, Bletchley, Roade, Northampton and Rugby widened lines opened goods. 31 Jul 1881 Bletchley to Roade passengers, 1 Dec 1881 Rugby to Northampton passengers, 3 Apr 1882 Roade to Northampton passengers.
2 Mar 1884	LNWR, Berkswell to Kenilworth Junction opened goods, 2 Jun 1884 passengers. Closed 18 Jan 1965 passengers, 17 Jan 1969 goods.
1 Mar 1888	LNWR, Weedon to Daventry opened. Closed 15 Sept 1958 passengers, 10 May 1964 goods.
18 Dec 1890	Harrow & Stanmore Railway, Harrow to Stanmore opened. Closed 3 Oct 1964.
13 Apr 1891	Easton Neston Mineral & Towcester, Roade & Olney Junction Railway, Towcester to Ravenstone Wood Junction with spur to LNWR at Roade opened goods. Spur at Roade closed 24 May 1917.
15 Jun 1912	LNWR, Watford to Croxley Green opened passengers, 1 Oct 1912 goods.
10 Feb 1913	LNWR, Watford to Willesden (New Lines), opened with services to Broad Street and Euston. Electric services provided 16 Apr 1917 Broad Street to Watford (via Hampstead Heath and Willesden), extended to Euston and Broad Street via Chalk Farm 10 Jul 1922. Dalston–Broad Street closed 27 June 1986, services diverted to Liverpool Street.
10 Aug 1914	LNWR, Coventry loop line opened. Humber Road Junction closed 10 Nov 1963.
1 Sept 1964	Steam locomotives banned south of Crewe.
3 Jan 1966	Electric services began from Euston.
6 Mar 1967	Full electric services provided to Birmingham New Street.
14 Oct 1968	New Euston Station officially opened.

London & Birmingham 2–2–0 passenger locomotive 28, built by Edward Bury. (Warwickshire County Library).

Rugby's second station in about 1850. (Warwickshire County Library).

Recovery work in progress at the derailment of the Irish Mail at Weedon on 14 August 1915. Looking south, Stowe Hill tunnel can be seen in the background. (Warwickshire County Library).

The erection of the 44 arm signal gantry across the main lines at Rugby in 1896 before the construction of the Great Central girder bridge. (Warwickshire County Library).

No 1997, an LNWR 4–6–0 19in Goods, a type used on local passenger and mixed traffic duties. (Warwickshire County Library).

Above:
The two Portland stone lodges, which date from about 1870, mark the entrance to Euston station on the Euston Road. Designed by the LNWR architect J. B. Stansby, the entrance lodges are among the few remaining relics of old Euston station.

Top left:
A 'small E class' 2–8–0 engine 2563 passing under the Great Central girder bridge at Rugby with an up goods. (Warwickshire County Library).

Left:
4–6–0 Claughton locomotive 161 normally used by the LNWR on London to Liverpool, Manchester and Glasgow services. (Warwickshire County Library).

Right:
On the top corner of each lodge can be seen the entwined letters of the LNWR monogram. Below are the names of the larger towns and cities that could have been reached from Euston. Beyond the lodges in the tree bordered Euston Square is the LNWR war memorial to 3,719 employees killed in the first world war.

A statue of Robert Stephenson, the builder of the London & Birmingham Railway, looks down on passengers entering Euston station. Sculptured by Carlo Marochetti the statue originally stood between the two lodges facing onto Euston Road before rebuilding of the terminus took place. New Euston station was opened by the Queen in 1968.

Two Class 86/2 locomotives stand at platforms 13 and 14. Passengers are boarding the coaches at platform 13 which formed the 15.05 to Liverpool on 13 September 1984.

13

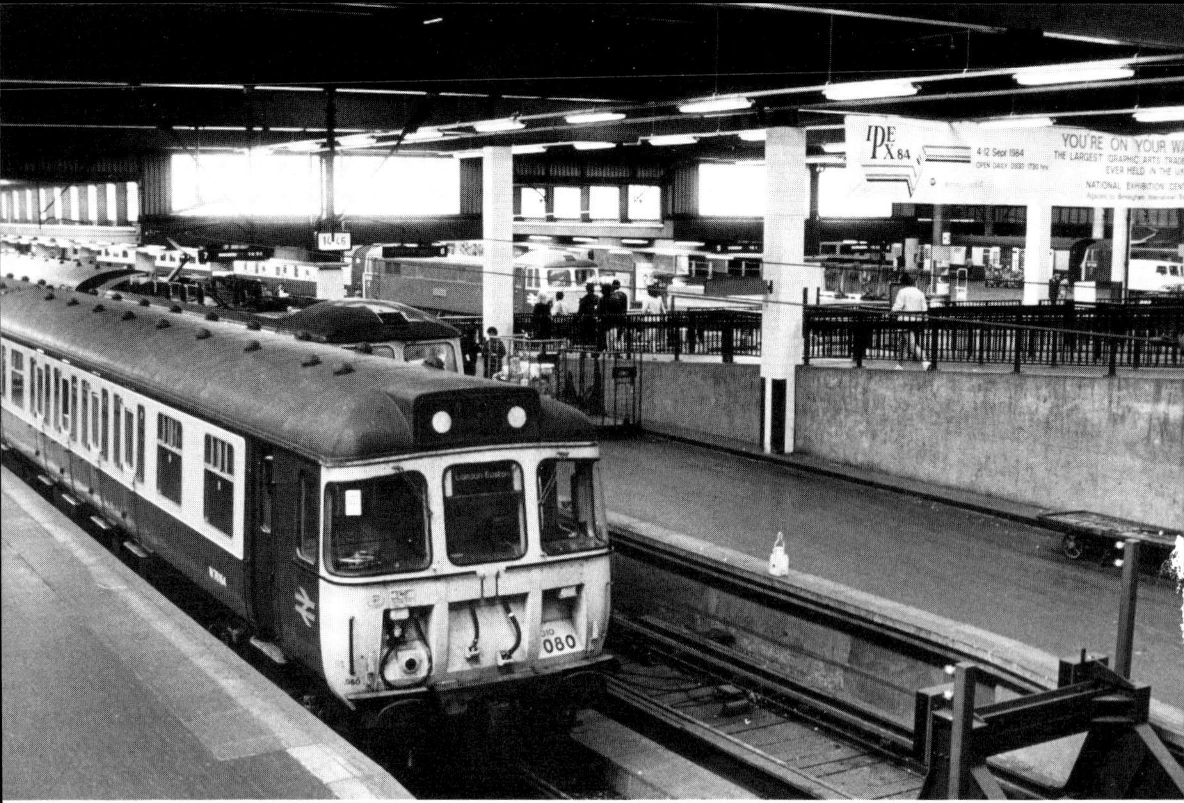
4-12 Sept 1984
London Euston
080

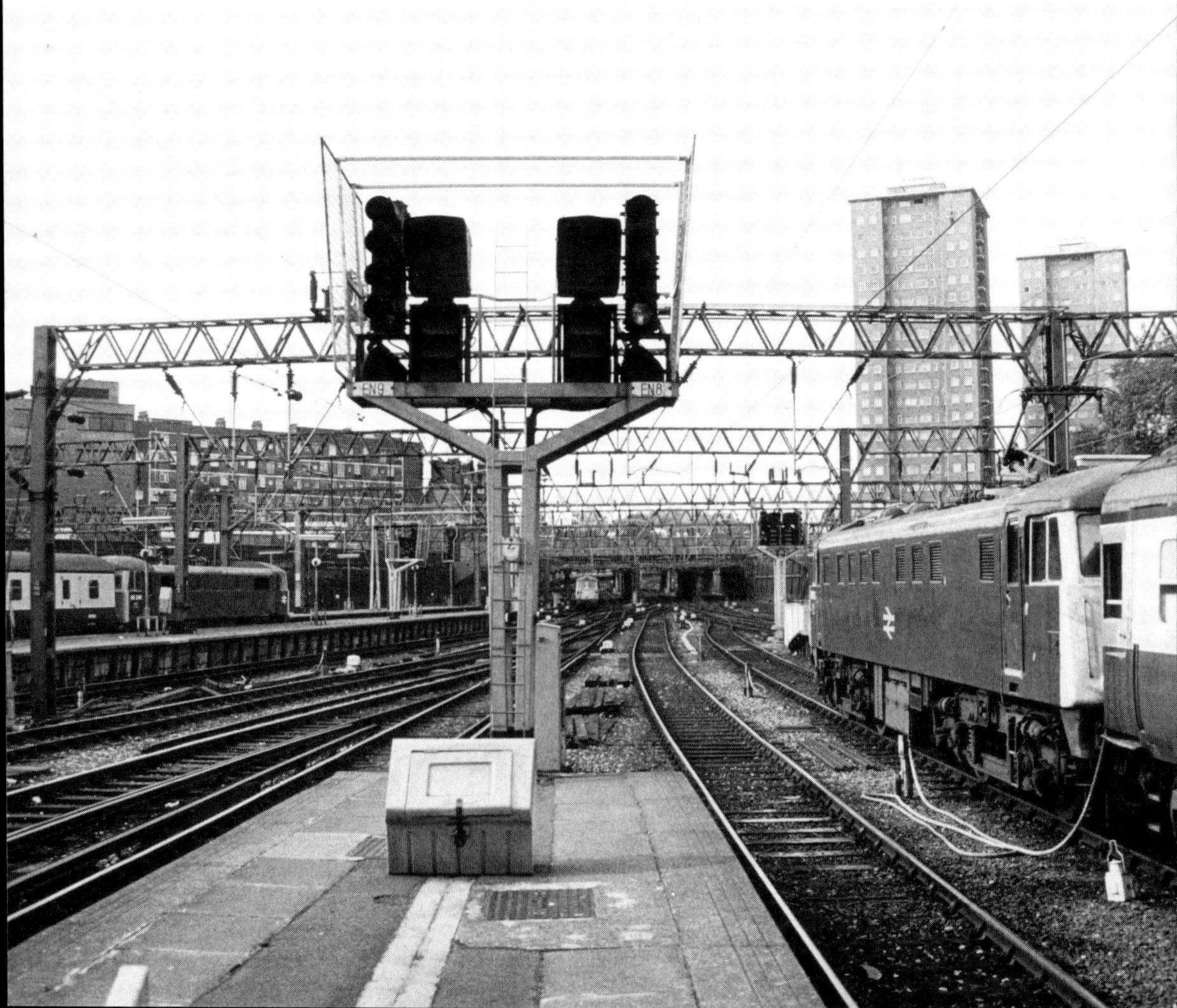
EN9
EN8

Mainstay of the London, Northampton, Birmingham semi-fast services is the four-car Class 310 electric multiple unit. No 310 080 and no fewer than three class 87 locomotives at Euston on 13 September 1984. Euston has 18 passenger platforms and three platforms specifically designed for parcels trains. However, changes in parcel carrying policy and alterations of other facilities have resulted in the parcels platform being used for other purposes including the West Coast Motorail service.

On the right No 81 013 prepares to take the 14.50 to Manchester and 86 246 waits with the 15.05 to Liverpool. A Class 87 stands below Hampstead Road bridge on 11 September 1984. From the north end of the platforms, between the heavy retaining walls, can be seen the start of the steep climb up to Camden.

Overhead electrical equipment obstructs the view of Euston from Hampstead Road as 86 257 *Snowdon* approaches the platforms on 13 September 1984.

At Camden, near the summit of the climb from Euston, the tracks cross Regents Canal – the canal itself causing problems for all three of the northern routes from London forcing the railway builders to go over or under. A sightseeing tourist boat named *Water Buffalo* passes along the canal towards Regents Park as a three coach Class 501 electric multiple-unit from Watford crosses the bridge to enter Euston. These units, introduced in the late 1950s gave way to Class 313 Units in 1986.

As the line curves round to the west, just north of the canal bridge, the first Camden depot was built on the east side of the line. The site of the depot is on the left of the picture. The whole depot covered an area of 30 acres and, apart from engine service facilities, provided warehousing for goods. On the right of the picture is the site of Camden shed which closed to steam in 1962.

Robert Stephenson's 1837 round house engine shed. The circular building of 160ft diameter built for 23 engines is positioned beside Chalk Farm Road just north of the original Camden depot site. After ceasing to have any railway use it became a theatre in the 1970s.

THE ROUND HOU
ACQUIRED BY CAMDEN
AS THE
HOME OF LONDON'S
BLACK ARTS

The track arrangement approaching the entrance to Primrose Hill tunnel dates from 1922. On 13 September 1984 No 86 243 *The Boys' Brigade* is approaching Euston on the up fast line at a point where it crosses both slow lines. A Freightliner train hauled by two Class 37 diesels can be seen moving on to the North London line tracks in the foreground, which lead to Camden Road and the Eastern Region.

A Class 86/2 enters Primrose Hill tunnel on the down fast line. Primrose Hill tunnels were constructed in three separate phases. The slow lines now occupy the original L&B tunnel. A second tunnel now used by the fast lines was completed in 1879. A full service into Euston through the third and fourth single line bores on the suburban electric system did not commence until 1922.

At the west end of Primrose Hill tunnel, a Class 501 electric unit arrives at South Hampstead station on 11 September 1984. The first station on this site with platforms on what are now the fast lines, was named Loudoun Road. It closed in 1917 and the present station was opened on 10 July 1922 on the electrified New Lines.

Kilburn High Road on a wet Sunday afternoon. The wooden canopy with its ornamental cast iron brackets which once graced the platforms has been removed. But at least the enclosed footbridge has been retained.

1959 Tube stock arriving at Queens Park from the Bakerloo line on 11 September 1984. The underground service reached Queens Park on 11 February 1915 forming a busy interchange between the LNWR suburban services and London's underground system. Bakerloo services were projected on over the LNWR New Line to Watford from 1917.

Kensal Green station is positioned at the entrance to the 966ft tunnel. The rebuilt station was opened in January 1981 and replaced the old LNWR structure at a cost of £250,000.

Built on the site of Willesden locomotive depot which closed in 1965, is the modern Freightliner depot with its huge container gantry crane.

On entering Willesden, the line passes the new locomotive maintenance depot on the up side. No 25 278 stands outside Willesden depot on a quiet Sunday afternoon, 7 October 1984.

No 86 257 *Snowdon* passes the site of Willesden Junction main line station on 7 October 1984. Willesden Junction station, with low level platforms and high level platforms serving Earls Court, and Broad Street–Richmond/Kew Bridge services was opened on 1 September 1866. Rebuilding followed in 1894, but after the second world war the large main line station was used only by suburban traffic. It was closed and demolished during the main line electrification programme in 1962.

A Class 501 multiple-unit at Harlesden working the 11.54 to Euston on 7 October 1984. The main line can be seen on the far left of the picture and, in the centre is the start of the extensive Willesden marshalling yard.

Just at the north end of Willesden yard the suburban New Lines pass under the main line on to the down side. A Class 501 multiple-unit emerges from under the main line on 6 October 1984 forming the 13.17 from Euston to Watford.

Southbound No 86 328 races through Wembley Central below the large High Road shopping centre on 11 September 1984.

A class 501 emu working the 11.36 to Watford waits in the dark and dismal Wembley Central station on 11 October 1984.

Passing Northwick Park is a Class 501 multiple-unit forming the 11.45 from Watford to Euston on 6 October 1984. In the background is the bridge carrying London Underground's Baker Street–Uxbridge/Amersham services and BR's Marylebone–Aylesbury line over the West Coast route.

WATFORD
B1

EUSTON
B1

Harrow and
Wealdstone
Trains
Car Park
Charges

Outer suburban emu No 310 094 forming the 15.19 to Euston waits at Harrow & Wealdstone on 6 October 1984. The centre section of the enclosed footbridge, over the fast lines, was demolished in the double collision which occurred at the station on 8 October 1952. In all 112 people were killed and ten died later from their injuries making this the worst railway accident in England. In the foreground is the bed of the former Stanmore branch line.

Harrow was the first place of any consequence outside London reached by the L&B, and the then small town was provided with an intermediate size station. A service of six up and six down trains ran in 1841. The 11½ mile journey from Euston took about half an hour. The present, elaborate Harrow & Wealdstone station designed by Gerald Horsley, was completed in 1912 together with the additional suburban New Lines and re-arranged fast and slow lines.

A Class 501 emu leaves Headstone Lane at 15.38 on 29 September 1984 for Euston.

The 11.02 Euston–Birmingham formed of emu No 310 074 passes Headstone Lane on 11 October 1984. Positioned alongside the down fast line, Headstone Lane has retained its attractive canopies and covered footbridge.

Within a few years of the line opening, an additional station named Pinner was provided. New platforms and station buildings designed by Gerald Horsley, were built in 1911 for the suburban services on the New Lines. Renamed Hatch End for Pinner, the resulting station approach and car park is far more impressive than most of the other stations on the suburban lines.

A Class 501 emu leaves Carpenders Park working the 14.32 to Watford on 29 September 1984. This station was originally built in 1914 as a wooden halt to serve a nearby golf course. Rebuilt in 1952, the timber from the old station was used to rebuild the platforms of Shefford station on the line from Bedford to Hitchin.

On Saturday 29 September 1984 multiple-units Nos 310 063 and 310 080 approach the site of Bushey water troughs forming the 12.30 Euston–Milton Keynes. Steam locomotives taking water at Bushey troughs were very popular subjects with railway photographers.

At Bushey station the lines of the suburban service make a sharp turn to the west away from the route of the main lines. On Saturday 29 September 1984 a Class 501 emu works the 12.51 to Euston.

WOLFF
WATFORD
82
CY
82

The first Watford station was opened to the public on 20 July 1837 when the L&B began services between Euston and Boxmoor. It was a principal grade station and the building, just north of the St Albans Road, is now used as offices. A new station was opened on its present site when the St Albans branch was opened in 1858.

Just south of Watford Junction the local dc electric lines rejoin the route of the main line. Multiple-units dominate the passenger services at Watford Junction. Three sets of Class 501 units stand in the terminal platforms. On the right is ac emu No 310 068 which with 310 066 formed the 10.51 to Milton Keynes on 11 October 1984. On the far right is a two-car Class 104 diesel multiple-unit, forming the 10.55 service to St Albans.

Watford Junction

Watford Junction station was extended over many years. A locomotive shed opened in the mid 1850s and closed in 1965. Diesel No 31 107 passes northwards through Watford with a freight working on 26 September 1984. Above can be seen two tower cranes being used in the construction of new station buildings.

After extensive reconstruction the new Watford station buildings were opened on 26 September 1985. The old 501 class suburban multiple units dating from the late 1950s have now been replaced with 313 class units from the Eastern Region. Unit No 313 008 stands at the new bay platforms beside the new station entrance on 25 May 1986.

No 86 312 with a BOC tank wagon train passes out of Watford tunnel on the down slow line on 26 September 1984. The tunnel, two miles north of Watford, was the only major construction on the L&B to be completed by the original contractor. However, there were some difficulties and one accident which claimed nine lives. In 1874 a second separate tunnel was opened to accommodate the slow lines.

Concrete and brick were used to build Apsley station which was opened by the LMS in 1938. The station of mulberry coloured brick, cream mortar and emerald window frames was built to cope with traffic from John Dickinson's mills and the expanding residential development in the area.

The first Boxmoor station opened as a temporary terminus on 20 July 1837. Later the station name became Boxmoor & Hemel Hempsted and today it is Hemel Hempstead. In the intervening years there were spelling changes in the name Hempstead. After the second world war Hemel Hempstead was designated a new town. Expansion, rebuilding and new housing followed, along with station rebuilding. Emu No 310 092 leaves Hemel Hempstead on 26 September 1984 forming the 13.04 to Milton Keynes.

87 030 *Black Douglas* races through Berkhamsted as emus Nos 310 060 and 310 076 leave as the 15.09 to Milton Keynes on 22 September 1984. The embankment on which the station stands, was built over marshland that took six months to drain with the aid of steam pumps.

Multiple-units Nos 310 076 with 310 060 forming the 13.48 to Euston wait at Tring beside the deserted carriage sidings. The section of line from Boxmoor to Tring was opened on 16 October 1837. After the turn of the century, Tring became an important terminus for outer suburban services from Euston and Broad Street. Gradually the Euston services were extended to Bletchley and today the new station at Milton Keynes has taken over much of this role.

North of Tring station No 86 257 *Snowdon* begins the descent through the 2½ mile Tring cutting on 22 September 1984.

No 85 004 passes through Tring cutting on the up fast line on 22 September 1984. The average depth of Tring cutting is 40ft but there is a quarter mile section which is almost 60ft deep. Apart from the catenary and additional tracks, this scene has changed little in 150 years. Even the copses of trees can be related to those shown in the Bourne lithograph of this area prepared at the time the line was built.

No 87 023 *Highland Chieftain* speeds through Cheddington station on 22 September 1984, past the platform which served the 1839 Aylesbury Railway, the first branch line to be built from the main line. In later years, despite competition for Aylesbury traffic from other more direct London routes, passenger services survived until 1953.

A principal grade station was opened at Leighton in April 1838 and in 1848 the seven-mile Dunstable branch opened. A through connection to Luton was made in 1858 and Leighton station was rebuilt in the following year. The station was renamed Leighton Buzzard in 1911 and the branch push and pull train continued in service until closure in 1962. Emu No 310 049 forming the 15.07 to Watford Junction and Euston waits on the up slow. To the right can be seen the old branch line platforms.

To the north of Leighton Buzzard is Linslade tunnel which consists of three separate bores. The central tunnel is the original L&B bore and the two outer tunnels were added in 1859 and 1876. A Class 86/2 locomotive and train emerge from Linslade tunnel on the down fast as another train enters the decorative northern portal. Enginemen on down expresses in steam days usually covered their heads as the locomotive entered the tight bore of the down fast tunnel to avoid the worst effects of swirling smoke, ash and soot created by the blast of the exhaust deflected back off the tunnel roof.

Bletchley station on 1 August 1984 as No 85 016 travels north on the down fast line with a Freightliner train. Bletchley first appeared in the timetable in June 1840, and in about 1851 an engine shed was opened. A retaining wall built of stone blocks from the old L&B trackway can be seen on the site of the shed which closed in 1965.

The branch to Bedford was opened in 1846. Another branch to Banbury opened in 1850 and to Oxford in 1951. An ageing Class 104 diesel unit arrives in Bletchley on 1 August 1984 forming the 16.15 from Bedford. Beside the Bedford line is the 1965 diesel and electric depot and in the background of the picture can be seen the overbridge which links the main line with the Oxford route.

Emu No 310 068 approaches Bletchley on 1 August 1984 on the up slow line. To the left can be seen the lines which climb up to the flyover to join the Oxford line.

Just north of Bletchley the line crosses Watling Street on a bridge of cast iron beams. From the north side of the bridge the original cast iron construction can clearly be seen.

On the south side of the bridge can be seen this commemorative inscription. From April to September 1838 most of the trains terminated near the bridge at a temporary station called Denbigh Hall. Stage coaches and up to 700 horses were provided to carry passengers from Denbigh to Rugby by-passing the incomplete section of the line at Blisworth and Kilsby.

The spacious entrance to Milton Keynes Central station which opened in 1982.

Emu No 310 053 forming the 14.57 from Birmingham to Euston leaves Milton Keynes on 1 August 1984.

Milton Keynes Central

Looking north from Blue Bridge the course of the original main line is on the left. Today's main line passes by the works on the right. The second Wolverton station of 1840 was positioned to the south of Stratford Road, on the left of the picture. To the east of the main line a branch was opened to Newport Pagnell in 1867 and closed in 1964.

No 85 015 approaches Wolverton on 31 July 1984. Wolverton is approximately midway between London and Birmingham and from the opening of the line it became the railway's locomotive centre. The tracks in the foreground are on the original L&B alignment which passed through the centre of the works. The present alignment dates from 1882 when the tracks were widened and diverted around the works.

Wolverton works on Stratford Road. The bogie shop, in the centre of the picture, was built in 1890. The works fire station still bears the letters LNWR above the appliance room doors.

The route of the old main line between the works buildings. On the left is the original workshop building constructed for the repair of locomotives and rolling stock. On the right is the workshop extension, built in 1845 for the erection of new locomotives. Before this the engines, all small four wheelers, had been supplied by Edward Bury, the locomotive superintendent, from his own factory in Liverpool.

In 1846, on the formation of the LNWR, Bury resigned and was replaced by J. E. McConnell who introduced larger, more powerful engines. In 1862, locomotive production was centred at Crewe, and in 1864 the LNWR concentrated all carriage work at Wolverton. Carriage construction ended in the mid 1960s, but repair work continued.

Wolverton station on 2 October 1984 with emu No 310 082 on the 16.30 Bletchley to Birmingham working. The wooden station buildings on the overbridge also served as the terminus of the 3ft 6in gauge Wolverton & Stony Stratford steam tramway.

Emu No 310 046, working the 13.02 Euston–Birmingham, on the curving Ouse embankment just north of Wolverton station on 27 October 1984.

WOLVERTON
082
Birmingham N St
046

No 86 312 *Elizabeth Garratt Anderson* passes the remains of Castlethorpe station on 1 August 1984. About a quarter of a mile south of the station were Castlethorpe water troughs. The station opened in 1882 and although closed in 1964 the stationmaster's house, the down fast and central island platforms remain.

Passing the site of Roade station is No 86 208 *City of Chester* on 16 July 1984. Only the booking office on the embankment now remains of the once busy station, which closed in 1964. However, there is a strong local movement trying to get a new station built with platforms on the slow lines.

No 86 224 *Caledonian*, in the middle of the cutting, approaches Roade on 30 August 1984. At this point, retaining walls have been built at both sides of the cutting. Stephenson maintained the stability of the narrow cutting by constructing inverts below track level.

On 30 August 1984, No 86 254 *William Webb Ellis* on the down slow line passes through the deep cutting between Roade and Blisworth. At 1½ miles long and up to 65ft deep, the cutting proved to be the most difficult of the earthworks on the line, taking 3000 barrels of gunpowder to blast away the rock.

From the north end of the cutting the extent of the earthworks and huge retaining walls can be seen. To improve the stability of the cutting and strengthen the retaining walls, a girder framework was constructed over the slow lines.

The line crosses the A43 road at Blisworth on a tall elegant single arch stone bridge from the original construction. Note the individually cut stones forming the arch. The first intermediate grade station at Blisworth was built beside this bridge.

From the north end of the Roade cutting the slow lines continue northwards towards Northampton while the fast lines turn towards Blisworth. No 87 018 *Lord Nelson* enters the cutting on the up fast line on 8 August 1984. The slow lines can be seen disappearing in the distance towards Northampton.

Passing north through the overgrown site of Blisworth's second station is No 86 240 *Bishop Eric Treacy* on 8 August 1984. In the foreground on the left is the site of some LNWR sidings and beyond, the start of the route to Peterborough. On the down side were exchange sidings, a signalbox, small engine shed and turntable used by the SMJ.

One of the prototype Advanced Passenger Train units, No 370 007 passes Banbury Lane Crossing on its return journey to Glasgow on 5 September 1984. Situated about 1½ miles north of the former Blisworth station, Banbury Lane signalbox still controls the level crossing barriers and associated signals.

The introduction of electric traction has reduced the risk of embankment fires and in places trees and bushes along the line side almost hide the railway from the surrounding countryside. No 86 030 curves south towards Blisworth with a parcels train on 19 September 1984.

One of the unusual methods of bridge construction used by Stephenson at a number of locations is the brick skew bridge. The brickwork beneath the arch shows the courses of bricks formed in a screw like pattern. To measure the angles of the stonework and brickwork courses a wooden model was constructed of each bridge. The details were then marked out on sheeting which was used to arrange the bricks on site.

Having emerged from Stowe Hill tunnel hidden in the mist, No 86 255 *Penrith Beacon* approaches Weedon on a misty morning in August 1984. It was on this section of the line that the down Irish Mail was derailed on 14 August 1915. A second accident occurred near this same section of track on 21 September 1951, when the leading bogie of a Princess class 4–6–2 working a Liverpool–London train derailed, damaging the track and most of the train was derailed.

No 87 009 *City of Birmingham* passes another Class 87 on the 80mph curved approach to Weedon.

G
68
41

One of the opponents of the railway was Squire Thornton of Brockhall. At the point nearest to his estate the line passes through a short cutting and the lineside fence was built beside the tracks at the bottom of the cutting so as not to spoil Thornton's view from the hall. Emu No 310 076 passes Brockhall heading for Birmingham on 3 August 1984, where the fence is still close to the line along the bottom of the cutting.

No 86 232 *Harold Macmillan* passes over the Grand Union Canal at Long Buckby Wharf on 18 July 1984.

A Class 87 locomotive passes the site of the first Weedon station. A principal grade station was provided at Weedon when the railway opened. A branch to Daventry and a new station north of the first opened in 1888. Very little evidence remains of the second station which closed in 1958, but a wall and part of a platform of the first station can still be seen.

Speeding south beside the M1 motorway near Watford Gap services is No 86 239 *L. S. Lowry* on 27 September 1984.

As the line turns away from the motorway it crosses the Leicester arm of the Grand Union Canal on a bridge of cast iron beams. The centre section of the bridge has been rebuilt with concrete but the original outer decorative cast iron beams and hand rails have been retained.

When the L&B opened, an intermediate grade station was provided near to the village of Watford, not to be confused with Watford Junction, but related to the Watford Gap services of the M1 motorway. The station was at first named Crick and later Welton. The close proximity of the Grand Union Canal resulted in Crick being used for the transfer of Midland coal from rail to canal from 1845. Today only the goods shed, decaying timber piles of the canal wharf and this row of railway houses remain.

No 86 313 leaves the southern portal of Kilsby tunnel on 12 September 1984. Construction of this tunnel, over 2,400yd long was the greatest challenge that faced Stephenson during the building of the L&B. Serious problems arose almost as soon as excavation of the first working shafts began, and on 30 November 1835 Stephenson deposited plans of a deviation to the line about one mile to the west. However, the deviation was not introduced and work continued on the original line.

To overcome fears of suffocation inside the tunnel, Stephenson built two of these huge 60ft diameter ventilation shafts. Both extend to a depth of over 100ft and are built of brickwork 3ft thick. The shafts are so large that at one time semaphore signals were installed inside them.

When the tunnel was nearing completion the engineering staff held a celebration at the Dun Cow, Dunchurch. The guests included the company chairman and George Stephenson.

A train hauled by a Class 86/2 locomotive approaches Kilsby tunnel from the north. On 21 June 1838 the tunnel was completed and a party of directors and engineers including George and Robert Stephenson complete with a band, marched through the tunnel to the north end where a celebration took place.

As the main line enters Rugby it is joined by the slow lines from Northampton at Clifton Mill Junction. On 15 July 1984 emu No 310 076 working the 14.15 from Euston approaches Rugby on the down slow while electric locomotive No 87 022 *Cock o'the North* crosses from the up fast to the up slow. This unusual track arrangement dates from the mid 1880s and was built by the LNWR to avoid conflict between trains on the main line and those from the Market Harborough branch and the slow lines. In the background of the picture can be seen the old Great Central girder bridge.

No 86 220 *Goliath* leaves Rugby on 15 July 1984 with the 15.11 to Manchester. This, the third Rugby station, was opened on 3 July 1885, and consists of one large island platform long enough to accommodate two main line trains on each side. A series of bay platforms were also provided to cope with the traffic from all of the lines that converged on the town.

Having by-passed the down platform, No 87 023 *Highland Chieftain* proceeds north from Rugby on 25 July 1984.

No 86 231 *Lady of the Lake* approaches Rugby on 27 July 1984 with the 15.18 Birmingham–Euston. This concrete viaduct carries the up line from Birmingham over the Trent Valley line avoiding conflict at the junction.

An intermediate grade station was opened at Brandon in 1838 but closure came in 1960. No 86 229 *Sir John Betjeman* speeds past the remains of Brandon & Wolston station on 11 September 1984 with the 14.18 Birmingham–Euston.

The approach to Coventry station from the east showing the loop line arrangements through the platforms. On the left, on the site of the old locomotive shed, is Coventry power signalbox.

Diesel locomotive No 47 257 crosses over the L&B route heading for Leamington with the 11.40 Manchester Piccadilly to Gatwick Airport via Oxford and Reading on 9 September 1984. After closure lasting 12 years, the Coventry Leamington line was reopened to passenger trains in May 1977.

Emu No 310 062, working the 19.10 for Birmingham and diesel locomotive No 47 144 stand at Coventry on 19 July 1984. The diesel locomotive is about to be changed for an electric locomotive. Since the reopening of the line to Leamington, Coventry has become a convenient point to change traction on many of the through services to non electrified lines.

A rather dirty No 86 207 *City of Lichfield* passes Canley with the 13.30 Wolverhampton to Euston on 28 August 1984. On the left can be seen the very small station building which dates from 1940.

A sunny morning greets No 47 354 as it leaves the western portal of Beechwood tunnel on 23 August 1984.

Canley
Beware
of trains

Berkswell

A freight train hauled by electric locomotive No 86 006 approaches Berkswell on 23 August 1984. In the foreground can be seen the remaining short section of a branch to Kenilworth which was opened in 1884 and closed in 1965.

Berkswell station, which dates from 1911, still retained its LNWR timber building on the down platform in 1984. A small halt named Dockers Lane was opened at this site in 1844 and the name Berkswell was not used until 1853.

Emu No 310 082 passes through Hampton-in-Arden on its way to London with the 1137 departure from Birmingham. Hampton-in-Arden was the only place of consequence between Coventry and Birmingham when the railway was first built and it was provided with an intermediate grade station.

In 1839 Hampton became a junction station with the construction of the Stonebridge Railway by the Birmingham & Derby Junction. The junction station was replaced in 1884 but the original building still exists and is now used as offices.

No 86238 *Lord Stamp* leaves Birmingham International with the 10.28 for Euston on 28 August 1984. To the east of the line is the National Exhibition Centre and to the west the International Airport.

Positioned close to trunk roads, motorways and airport, Birmingham International, which opened in 1976, is an important bus-rail-air interchange point.

The new airport terminal which was opened in 1984 is linked to the station by a MAGLEV passenger transport system on an elevated trackway.

Emu No 312 202 forming the 11.23 to Birmingham waits for late passengers at Marston Green on 28 August 1984. This station has been provided with rail-bus interchange facilities and in 1984 new station buildings were being erected.

Emu No 312 202 working the 14.26 to Birmingham arrives at Lea Hall on 16 May 1986. This station was first opened in 1939 during extensive residential and industrial development in the area.

About to leave Stechford is No 310 085 as the 11.59 for Birmingham New Street on 28 August 1984. Stechford is the junction between the L&B line and the Grand Junction route to Wolverhampton which avoids Birmingham.

Leaving Adderley Park on 28 August is emu No 310 085 as the 12.25 to Coventry. Tickets were not collected or checked at the old New Street station. Ticket collectors boarded trains approaching Birmingham at Adderley Park to collect tickets before they reached New Street.

As the line emerges from the Adderley Park cutting it passes Lawley Street Freightliner terminal which occupies the site of the short lived Birmingham & Derby Junction terminus.

The first Birmingham terminus of the L&B was at Curzon Street. Designed by Philip Hardwick the monumental station portico is still strikingly impressive, symbolising the proud ambitions of the railway.

Emu No 310 062 climbs out of Birmingham New Street on 7 September 1984 between the heavy retaining walls.

An arrangement of the L&B heraldic device still decorates the entrance doorway to the Curzon Street station building. After closure to passengers the old station was used as a goods terminal for over 100 years. Restoration eventually followed and in 1984 the project received a conservation award from the Royal Institution of Chartered Surveyors.

A Class 87 light locomotive about to enter New Street South tunnel. Above can be seen the Rotunda building and the canopies of Moor Street station. Just over the entrance to the tunnel is the bridge which carried the Great Western tracks to Snow Hill.

Emerging from South tunnel and entering New Street platforms is emu No 310 060 working the 12.02 from Euston on 7 September 1984. New Street station was opened on 1 June 1854. The roof was about 840ft long with a span of 209ft, the largest ever built until the Midland Railway opened St Pancras in 1868.

Electric locomotive No 86 248 *Sir Clwyd/County of Clwyd* and multiple-unit No 310 060 wait at Birmingham New Street on 7 September 1984. During the rebuilding of New Street in the 1960s, twelve through platforms were provided and on a concrete raft above the platforms are positioned the station offices, booking hall and ticket barriers, and a shopping precinct.